**Synth Evolution V**

The first two volur
synthesizers, drum
and 1980s. Volume three moves us into the 21st century, and is a selection of some of the most interesting, impactful and – arguably - best synthesizers from the past two decades.

Of course, any selection will necessarily not be exhaustive, and I've had to make some difficult choices. I apologise if your personal favourite is missing - but let me know and we'll see what we can do for future volumes!

The synths in this book celebrate the range of sonic possibility now available to musicians and producers in the modern age. There's everything from analogue wonders to extraordinary digital creations; from tightly designed monosynths to open-ended polyphonic beasts. Each one more marvellous than the last.

A shout to my good friend Rafael Szaban who has more synth knowledge in his little finger than I could ever hope to learn, and with whom I very much enjoyed discussing and debating the shortlist. Obviously, any choices you disagree with were entirely my doing. Prices shown were those at launch.

Vive le synth!

# Access Virus TI2

## 2009 / £1,895

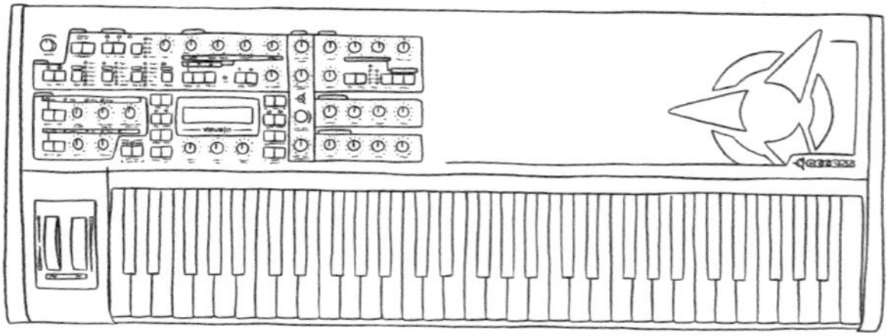

The Virus series, launched by German firm Access in 1997, was a breakthrough in virtual analogue synthesis. By 2009, the series had reached its pinnacle with the TI2. While the core virtual analogue technology remained a constant, each iteration of the Virus improved upon the last, introducing new features, additional oscillators, and increased polyphony.

Its punchy, clean sound and powerfully resonant filters maintained its popularity throughout its lifespan, with TI2 production continuing until 2024 - a remarkably long run for any synthesizer.

Virtual Analogue / 80 Voice / 3 Osc + Sub

# Alesis A6 Andromeda

## 2000 / £2,599

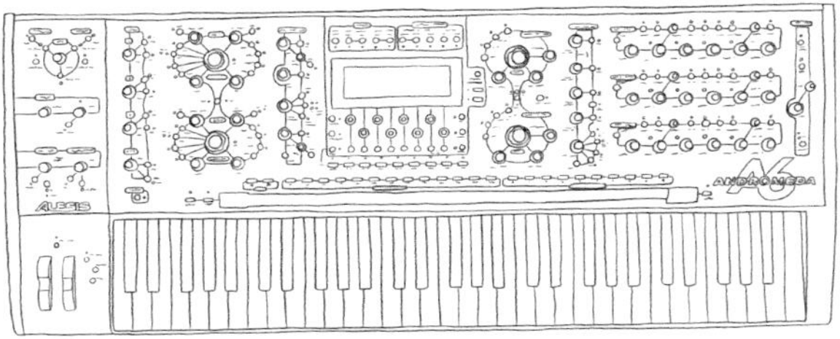

This imposing machine is a sixteen-note polyphonic analogue beauty with two oscillators and two resonant multi-mode filters per voice. The filters themselves are modelled on the vintage sound of the Moog Modular 904 and Oberheim SEM.

With ring modulation, hard-sync, arpeggiator, digital effects and a comprehensive modulation matrix, this is a modern pan-galactic classic.

Analogue / 16 Voice / 2 VCOs + Sub

# Analogue Solutions AS100 Colossus

2019 / £26,900

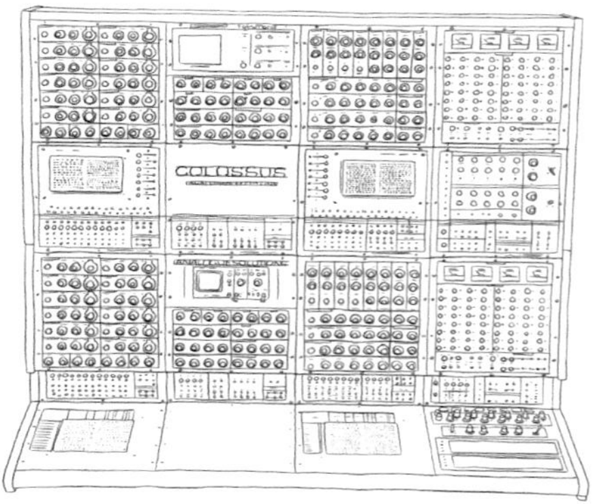


The AS100 Colossus features twelve VCOs, two LFOs, four VCAs, eight VCFs, two noise generators, four envelopes and two ring modulators....oh, and two (two!) spring reverbs. And a 64-note step sequencer.

It's inspired by the classic EMS Synthi 100 of the 1970s but is in no way a clone. This is a machine for those with the budget to match their passion for a modern take on vintage analogue!

Analogue / 12 VCOs

# Analogue Solutions Leipzig S

2012 / £800

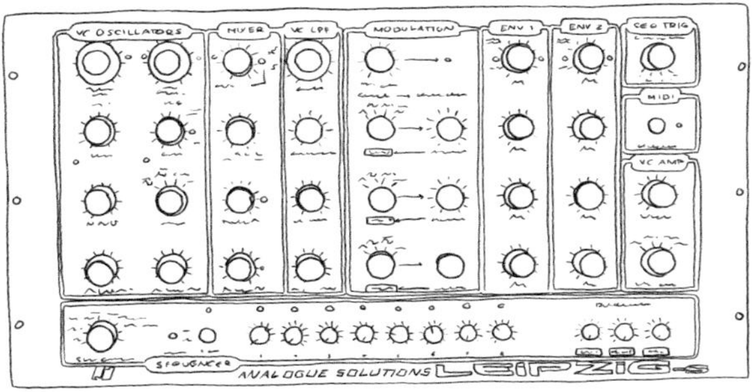


In contrast with the Colossus's colossal cost, the Leipzig S is practically a budget synth and is prized for its raw and beefy sound. Its two main oscillators may seem limited by offering only sawtooth and square wave options, but they are boosted by the addition of a sub-oscillator, hard-sync and frequency modulation making for a large range of gnarly tones.

Coupled with the Moog-esque resonant filter and a sixteen-note step sequencer, this is one of the most desirable monosynths of the last 25 years.

Analogue / Monosynth / 2 VCOs + Sub

# Arturia MiniBrute

## 2012 / £429

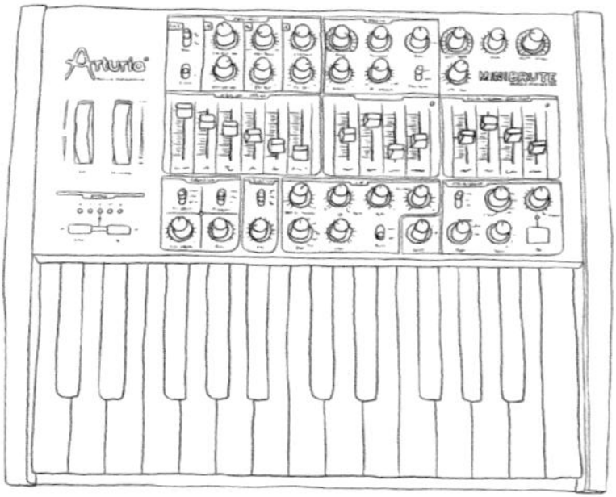

The Arturia 'Brute' series has been a staple of the synth scene since 2012, and was the first hardware from Arturia after years of soft synths. While it features only one VCO, that single oscillator includes a sub, and its four waveforms - sawtooth, pulse, triangle, and noise - can be layered with additional wave-shaping options.

The filter is a Steiner-Parker multi-mode design (first used on the legendary Synthacon in 1979), adding a unique character, while the 'Brute Factor' loops audio back into the filter's signal path for maximum Brutishness.

Analogue / Monophonic / 1 VCO + Sub

# Arturia PolyBrute

## 2020 / £2,259

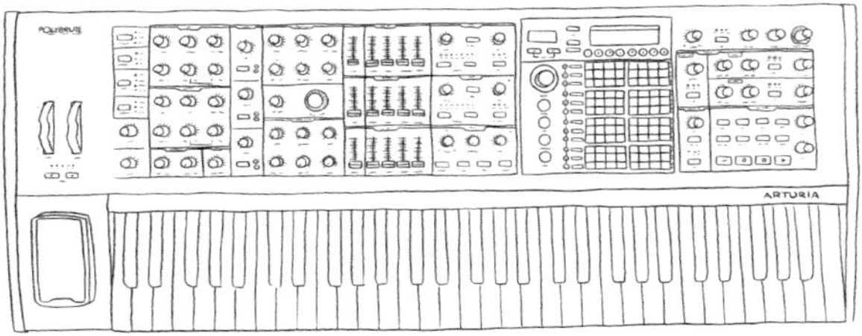

The MiniBrute on steroids! The tasty-but-monophonic Mini has grown into a six-note PolyBrute beast. It retains the four waveshapes per oscillator which can be layered simultaneously, and adds a 32-note arpeggiator and 64-note step sequencer.

The distinctive modulation matrix offers extensive routing possibilities, and like the MiniBrute, the multi-mode Steiner-Parker and ladder filters can feedback audio from the output back to the input for increased brutality!

All this must have contributed to its win of 2022's Sound On Sound best synth award!

Analogue / 6 Voice / 2 VCOs + Sub per Voice

# ASM Hydrasynth

## 2019 / £1,299

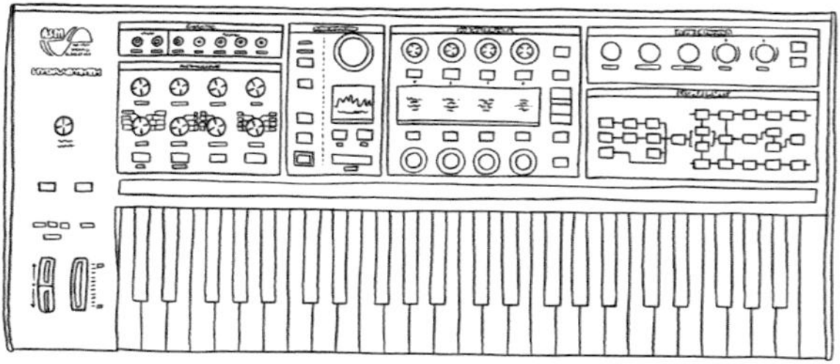

The highly-anticipated Ashun Sound Machines' Hydrasynth was the first synthesizer to bring back true polyphonic aftertouch since the Yamaha CS-80 of 1977, taking advantage of the MIDI Polyphonic Expression (MPE) spec of 2018.

It did not disappoint - each of its eight notes of polyphony is created by three digital oscillators and each sports additional 'mutators' which provide linear FM, wave-stacking, hard sync, PWM and a 'harmonic' manipulator.

Capable of rich analogue sounds and exotic digital creations, the subsequent models include the smaller Hydrasynth Explorer and the flagship 73-note Hydrasynth Deluxe.

Digital / 8 Voice / 3 Osc per Voice

# Buchla Easel Command 208c

## 2020 / £3,000

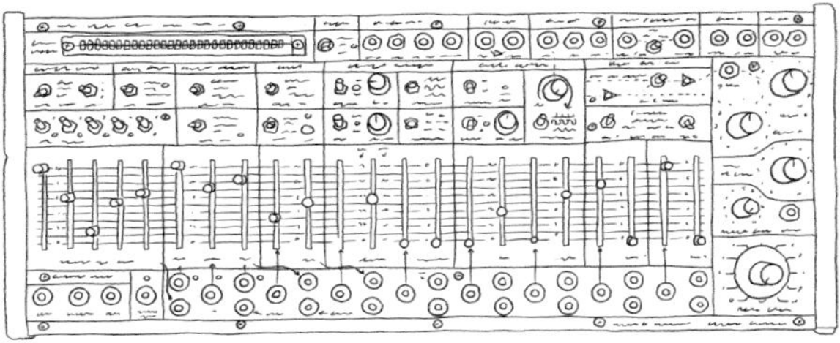

Don Buchla was a pioneering West Coast synthesizer designer who developed some of the earliest modular synths in the 1960s (while Robert Moog was simultaneously crafting his own approach to modular synthesis on the East Coast.)

The Easel Command 208c is an updated version of the classic 1972 Music Easel which encapsulates the essence of Buchla's design ethos: complex harmonic oscillators with less reliance on filters (in contrast to the subtractive synthesis of the east coast); a ban on piano-style keyboards, and a desire to approach electronic music with a truly open mind.

Analogue / Monophonic / 2 VCOs

# Clavia Nord Lead 3

## 2001 / £1,899

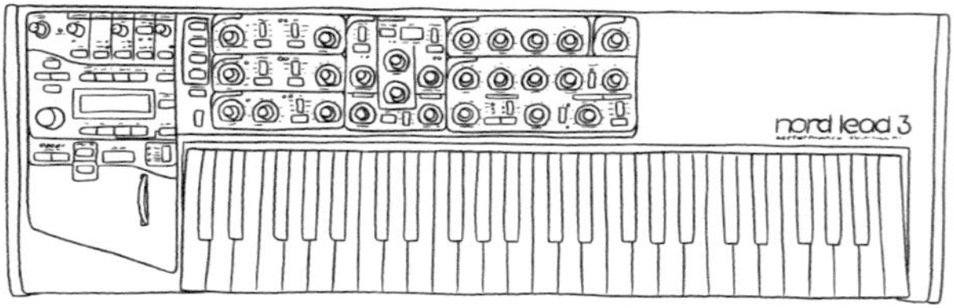


Clavia's strikingly red Nord Lead series reached its third incarnation in 2001. The first two are arguably the classic Leads from the sonic perspective, but this one is prized for its LED rotary controls indicating each patch's starting position - and still sounds amazing!

Polyphony is up to 24 voices, with FM synthesis, wave-shaping, and multiple types of distortion modulation.

The Nord Lead series has been an iconic mainstay of the serious musician's sonic arsenal since its introduction in 1995.

Virtual Analogue / 24 Voice / 2 Osc per Voice

# Cwejman Sound S1 MkII

## 2004 / £2,000

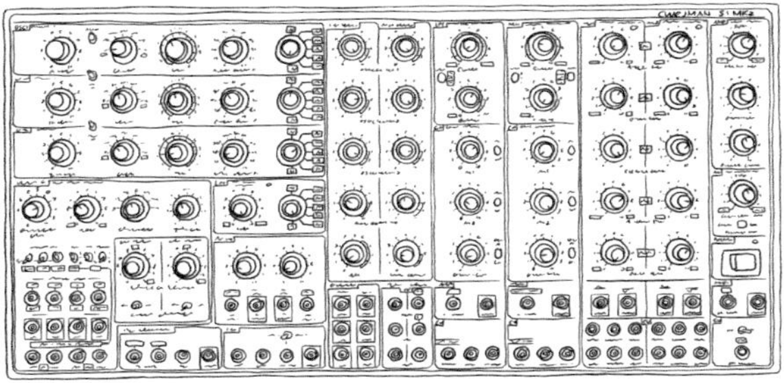


Cwejman, a Swedish company founded by brilliant Polish synth designer Wowa Cwejman, has been crafting analogue synthesizers since the 1970s.

The S1 MkII is a standout in the lineup, offering incredible versatility through its semi-modular architecture. It features two multi-mode filters with overdrive, ring modulation, a noise source, and cross-modulation enabling rich FM tones and a powerful oscillator sync.

Analogue / Monophonic / 3 VCOs

# Dave Smith Instruments Evolver

## 2002 / £350

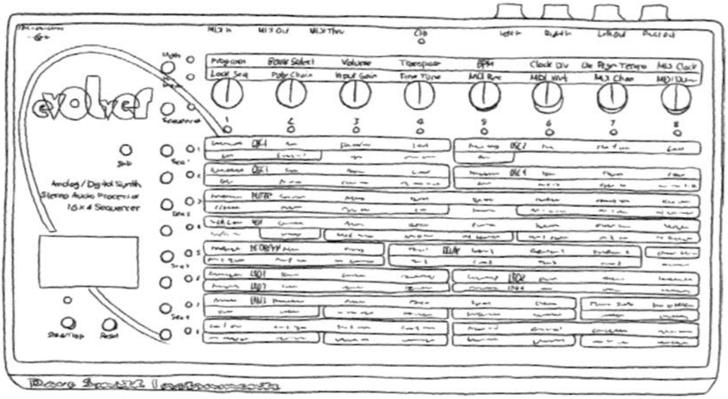


After a time working in software synthesis in the 1990s, Dave Smith returned to hardware design with the Evolver wavetable synth in 2002. It's a monosynth with an impressive - but unusual - combination of two analogue and two digital oscillators. The analogue oscillators are capable of saw/triangle/variable pulse and can be hard-synced; the digital oscillators feature the waves from the Prophet VS.

As its name suggests, it excels in wavetable sequencing and evolving sounds, combining the best of analogue and digital. Despite sounding great, it was criticised at launch for being relatively hard to program.

Analogue & Digital Wavetable / Monophonic / 4 Osc

# Dave Smith Instruments Sequential Prophet 6

2015 / £1,999

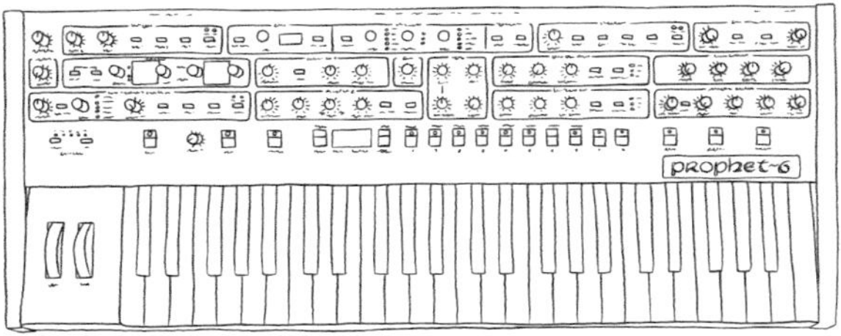


Once Ikutaro Kakehashi of Roland graciously returned the Sequential name to Dave Smith in 2015, the stars aligned and the world welcomed the return of the true (analogue) Prophet.

Building on the architecture of the Prophet 5, the '6' adds more modulation routing, audio-rate LFOs, positive/negative envelopes for the filter envelope (the 5's were only positive), arpeggiator, sequencer, effects and more.

Put all that together and you have the first genuine, stable and vaguely affordable Prophet synthesizer for 41 years!

Analogue / 6 Voice / 2 VCOs + 1 Sub per Voice

# Dave Smith Instruments OB6

2016 / £2,499

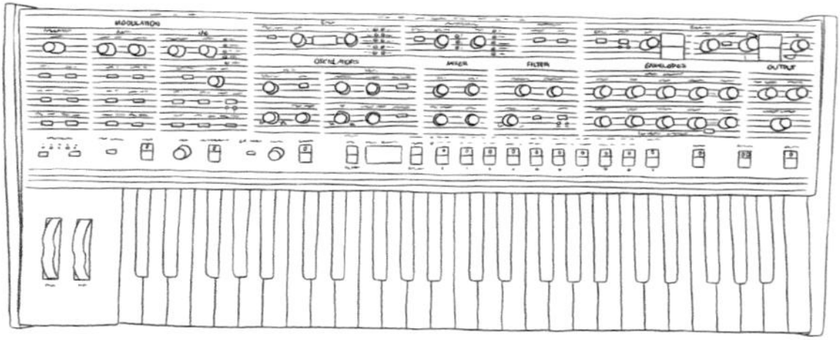

A collaboration between the legends Dave Smith and Tom Oberheim with the aim of creating a latter-day polyphonic Oberheim SEM synth. The OB6 is based on the earlier DSI Prophet 6 chassis but with all-new Oberheim SEM-style voice cards and filters.

It may not be a direct clone of an Oberheim OB classic, but by modernising the VCOs, and offering Prophet 6-style features such as cross-modulation, this succeeded in nailing the classic Oberheim sound - and much more besides.

Analogue / 6 Voice / 2 VCOs per Voice

# Doepfer Dark Energy

## 2009 / £349

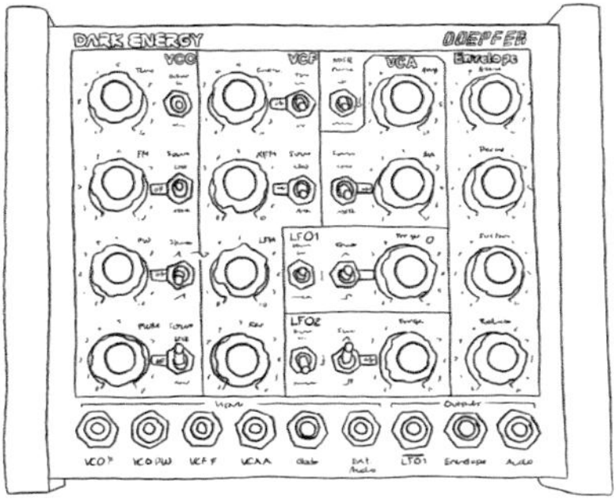


The instigators of the modern Eurorack phenomenon produce their first standalone synth (equivalent to their A-115 Mini Synthesizer module). Modest at first glance with only one VCO, the Dark Energy is a good deal more versatile than one might expect.

The Curtis CEM3394 VCO combines a square wave with either a triangle or sawtooth wave and the FM-capable LFO pushes the filter into more exotic sonic territory.

Additionally, the highly flexible modulation routing makes this a nicely creative monosynth.

Analogue / Monosynth / 1 VCO

# Elektron Monomachine SFX6

2004 / £1,300

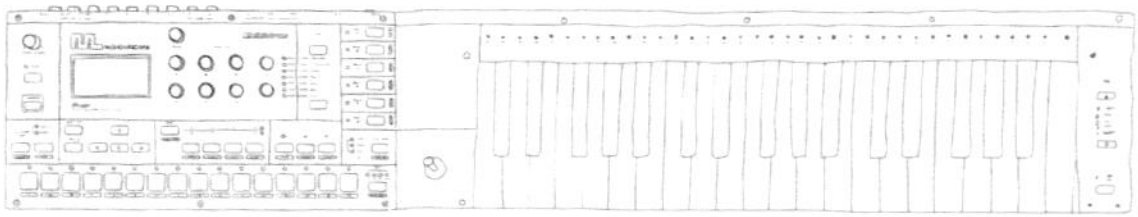

The unusual looking Monomachine SFX6 was Elektron's follow-up to the well-regarded SIDstation and MachineDrum, and incorporates aspects of both.

There are six different oscillator types to choose from - a virtual analogue oscillator, a SID-chip emulator, a wavetable synth, a choice of sampled percussion, FM, vocal formant modelling and an effects section. And a six-track sequencer!

The Monomachine is an idiosyncratic machine (which isn't actually mono at all, of course; and available as a standalone module), and which paved the way for future Elektron devices such as the Octatrack, Digitakt and more.

Digital / 6 Voice / Variable Osc per Voice

# Expressive E Osmose

## 2023 / £1,659

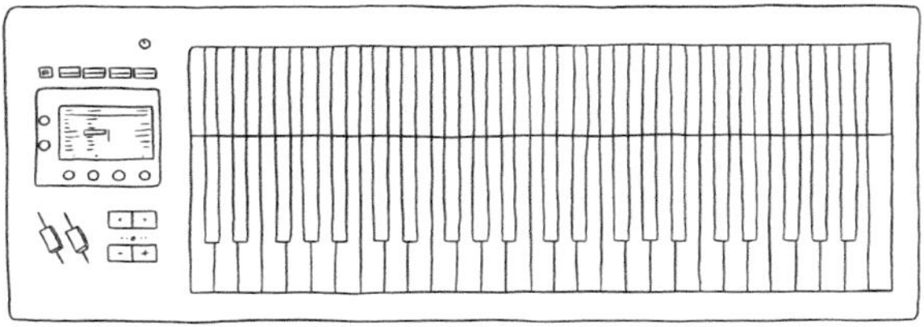

Few manufacturers dare step beyond the limitations of the conventional piano keyboard, but Expressive E are amongst their number.

The Osmose is arguably one of the most successful to attempt an upgrade to the piano-style keyboard, with its combination of unique side-to-side key movement and detailed vertical travel. Its powerful MPE-supporting EaganMatrix synth engine is capable of virtual analogue, FM, physical modelling and granular synthesis.

Digital / 24 Voice / 5 Oscillators + Noise

# Future Retro 777

## 1998 / £499

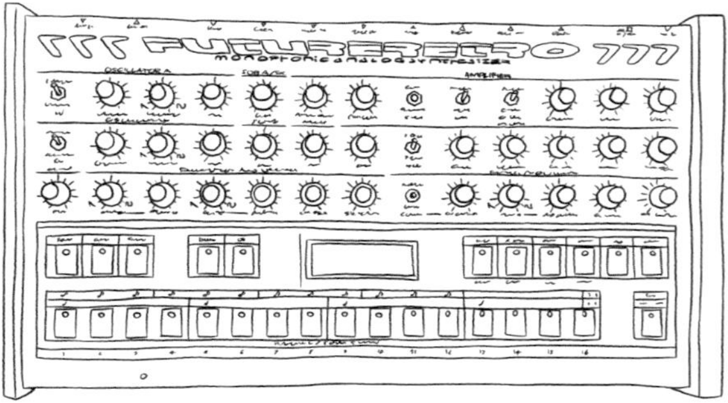

The 777 has snuck into this volume as it's much more than just another TB-303 clone. Yes, it can bang out 303 basslines no problem, but it can go so much further.

It has two oscillators with sub (compared to the 303's one lonely oscillator) and replicates the accent and glide of the original. The filter also includes an overdrive option and there is a 16-note step sequencer. Armed with all this, there's no acid house party that couldn't be improved with a 777!

Analogue / Monophonic / 2 VCOs + Sub

# Groove Synthesis
# 3rd Wave

2023 / £4,000

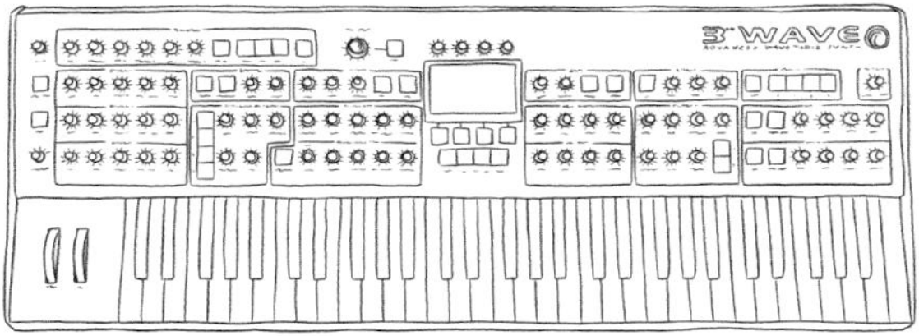


A straight-up homage to the revered PPG Wave 2, even down to the original's striking blue colour.

It comes with the 32 eight-bit wavetables of the original PPG, and there are 64 user locations for new high-resolution 96kHz waves. Like the original, the filters are analogue and fully self-oscillating, and there is also oscillator-sync, linear FM and of course, extensive modulation possibilities - splendid for wave-table modulation.

Lead designer Bob Coover has previously worked with Dave Smith on the Prophet 12, OB6, and more, so this synth is assuredly of the highest quality.

Digital Wavetable / 24 Voice / 2 Osc per Voice

# Hartmann Neuron

## 2003 / £3,499

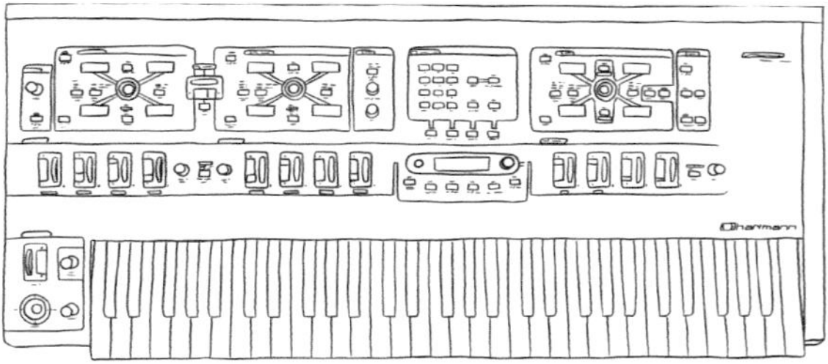


More of a curiosity than a classic if we're to be honest, but 2003 is pretty early for what is essentially an 'AI synth'. More technically the Neuron was a 'resynthesis synth', creating a mathematical model of a sample using neural net technology. This, in theory, allowed for deeper, more naturalistic sound manipulation than conventional sample editing.

However, in practice, the synth itself was perhaps too advanced for the technology of the time, and despite support from Hanz Zimmer, it was not quite ready to herald a new age of synthesis.

Digital / 8 Voice / 2 Resynators per Voice

# John Bowen Solaris

## 2011 / £3,999

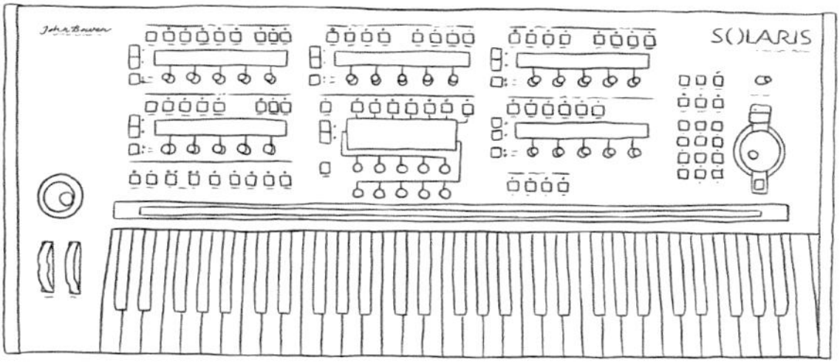


Originally a VST by John Bowen—formerly of Korg and Creamware—the Solaris is a highly ambitious synthesizer with ten voices, each featuring up to four oscillators. These oscillators are true chameleons, capable of emulating the Minimoog and Oberheim SEM, replicating the Prophet VS, acting as wave-shaping oscillators, functioning as multi-mode oscillators, supporting wavetables (with Waldorf tables), and even operating as sample playback oscillators.

There isn't enough space to discuss the 36 filter types, audio-rate 'rotor' blending, amplitude modulation, and all the other unique and extraordinary things that embody this very unusual synthesizer.

Digital / 10 Voice / 4 Osc per Voice

# Korg Karma

## 2001 / £1,599

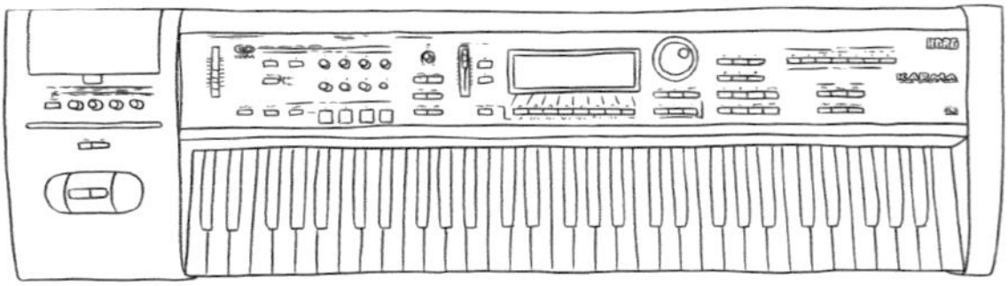

A rare entry in the unfashionable 'ROMpler Synth' category, Korg built on their well-respected Triton workstations with the KARMA and its innovative 'Generated Effects' system.

The GE System manipulates notes in real-time - whether through delays, pitch shifts, drum patterns, or melodic riffs. Designed by Stephen Kay (leading to the acronym, '**K**ay's **A**lgorithmic **R**eal-time **M**usic **A**rchitecture'), the KARMA aimed to support a more naturalistic playing style.

Sample & Synthesis / 62 Voice / 2 Samples per Voice

# Korg MS2000

2000 / £600

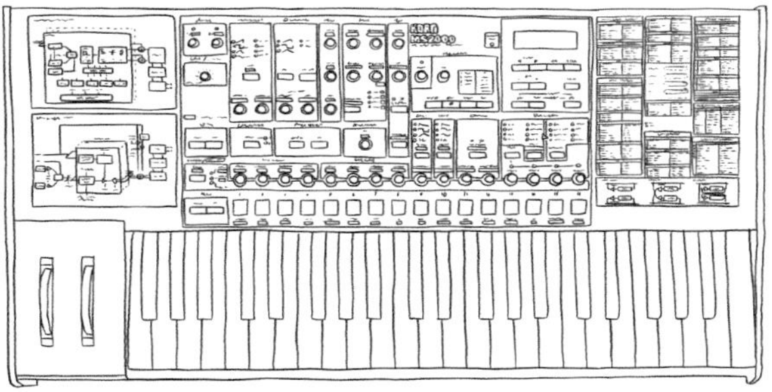

The MS2000 is a virtual analogue modelling synth whose name deliberately references the Korg classics - MS-10, MS-20 and MS-50, and it retains its reputation to this day.

With only four-note polyphony (perhaps a limitation which is an inadvertent homage to the Korg Mono/Poly), it still had a sound that was highly prized.

It sported a pleasing look that referenced the vintage synths of the 1970s and represented a fresh start for Korg in the 21st century.

Virtual Analogue / 4 Voice / 4 Osc

# Korg microKorg

## 2003 / £399

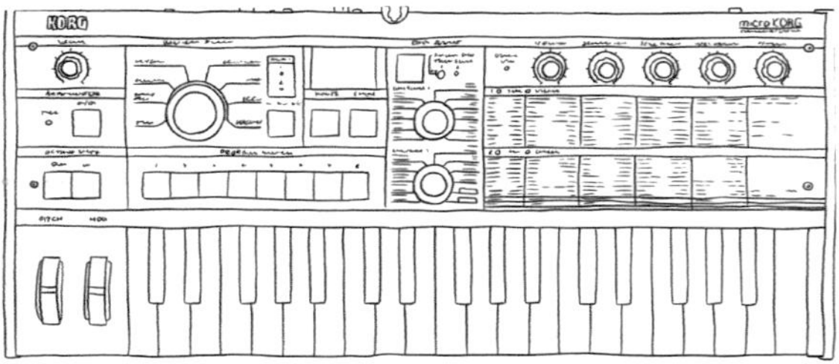

A true modern classic based on the well-respected MS2000. This four-oscillator analogue-modelling synth also boasts a vocoder - as did the MS2000 - which was pretty nifty in the heyday of Daft Punk and others. Its four oscillators could be run in four-voice polyphonic mode, duophonic mode or one mighty unison mode.

Despite mini-keys and being slightly awkward to program, its sound is what has kept it in high regard - and in production - for over 20 years.

Virtual Analogue / 4 Voice / 4 Osc

# Korg Volca Series

From 2013 / £139-159

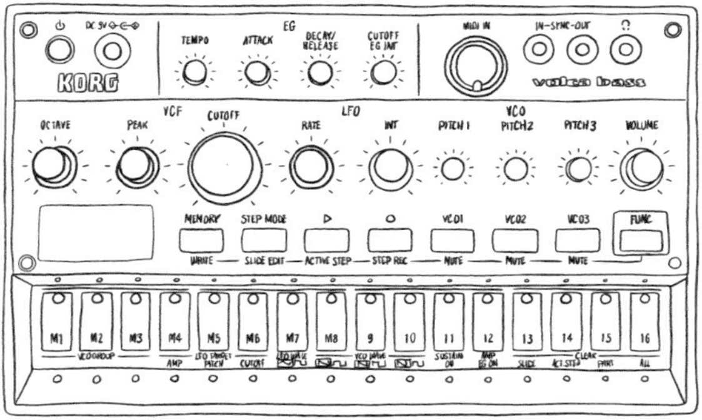


Korg's cool little volca boxes started appearing in 2013 in the now familiar 'glorified matchbox' form factor. Each volca focuses on one type of synthesis or sound type and does it simply, effectively and affordably.

Consequently, they've been a huge hit and you just have to 'catch them all'!

In the series so far: bass (pictured), keys, beats (2013), sample (2015), kick (2017), mix (2018), modular, drum (2019), nubass (2020), sample 2 (2021), fm 2 (2022).

# Macbeth M3X

## 2002 / £880

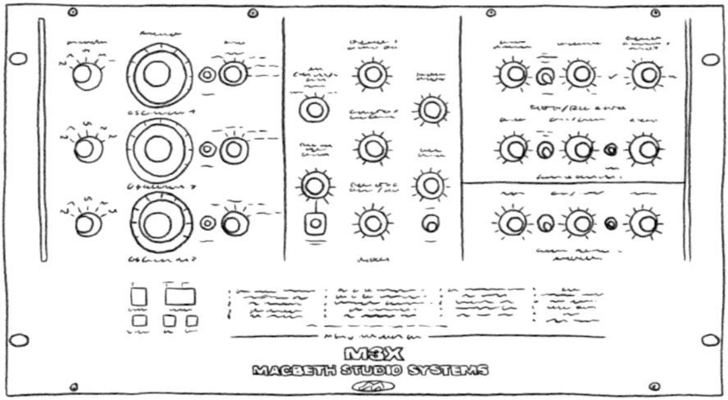


The first synth from highly respected Scottish synth designer, Ken MacBeth, and still sounding great. Modelled on the Minimoog, the M3X adds extra touches like second oscillator pitch modulation, FM, and a fully positive/negative filter envelope.

Whilst it can replicate the sound of a Minimoog, it can also go much, much further. An updated M3X2 was released in 2006, with extra patch-points and a temperature-compensated filter resonance allowing for 10-octave accurate tracking.

Analogue / Monophonic / 3 VCOs + Noise

# Make Noise 0-Coast

## 2016 / £449

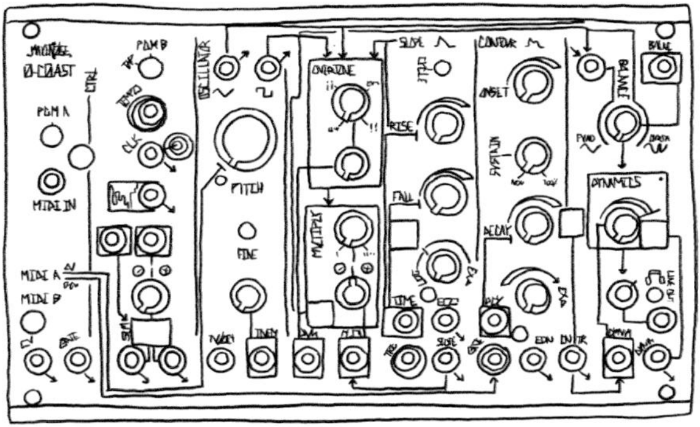


A synth capable of a stunning range of sounds that belies the fact it only has one oscillator. Through its use of extreme harmonic manipulation, wave cycling, slope mod, LFO, and linear FM, it can generate a great deal of sonic complexity.

Despite the name '0-Coast' suggesting no affiliation to either east or west coast synthesis, the reality is that this is very much in the Buchla mould: complex oscillators and no low-pass filtering to smooth out the resulting joyous, audiophonic chaos!

Analogue / Monophonic / 1 VCO

# MFB Dominion 1

## 2014 / £1,200

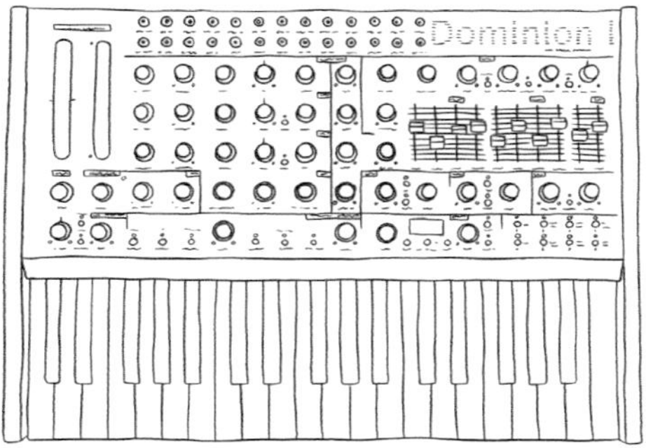


The MFB Dominion 1 stakes its claim as the ultimate monosynth—a bold assertion maybe, but one that might be justified by its meticulous design and immense sonic versatility.

It features three oscillators, each with an impressive seven-octave range and a precise thirteen-semitone fine-tune control. The analogue filters offer twelve modes, and nearly every parameter is open to modulation - even the filter resonance.

With FM capabilities, three audio-rate LFOs that reach up to 1.2 kHz, an arpeggiator, and a 128-step sequencer, this synth has it all going on!

Analogue / Monophonic / 3 VCOs + Noise

# Modal Cobalt 8

## 2021 / £579

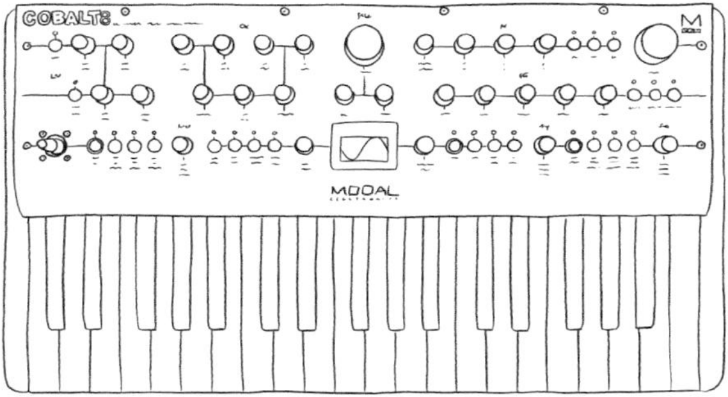


The Cobalt 8 is a classy virtual analogue synth with eight-note polyphony and a nice line in oscillators. The oscillator algorithms range from the expected saw, square, and sine to more exotic options such as wave-folding, ring-modulation, and 'fractal' waves.

Sound sculpting is cleverly done with two macro parameters per oscillator, each tailored to the selected algorithm giving the most useful control without being overwhelmed with options.

Virtual Analogue / 8 Voice / 2 Osc per Voice

# Moog MiniMoog Model D (Reissue)

2016 / £3,599

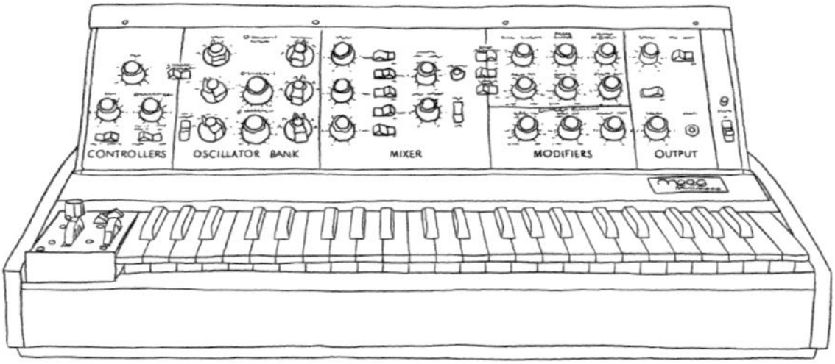


Is this really a 'modern classic' given it was designed over 50 years ago? I don't care! If Moog is going to re-release the Minimoog Model D to this level of perfection, to the extent that it's basically just a continuation of the original production run - albeit with a trifling 35-year hiatus - then I'm not going to complain.

It's a new Minimoog Model D. Made by Moog. End of!

Analogue / Monophonic / 3 VCOs + Noise

# Moog One

## 2019 / £5,999-£7,999

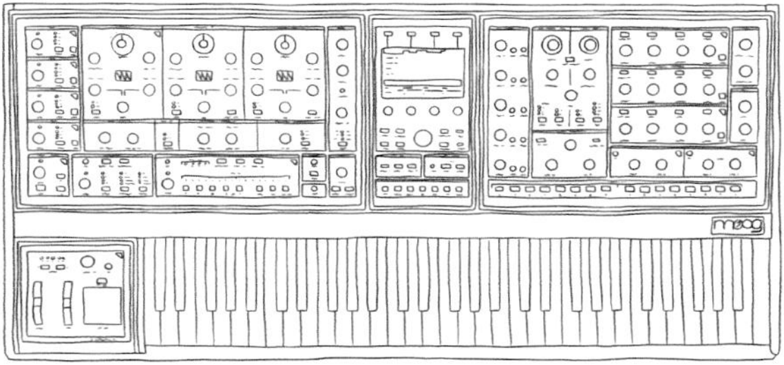


Moog's flagship synthesizer roars into the spotlight and does not disappoint. A true analogue thoroughbred lovingly designed for the best possible synthesizing experience.

It's wrapped in a beautiful wooden case with 200 dedicated controls on the surface - and, of course, most importantly - delivers that classic Moog sound. Three oscillators per voice (each with its own multimode or ladder filter), extensive modulation options, FM, and much more.

SOS Synth of the Year 2019, say no more!

Analogue / 8 or 16 Voice / 3 VCOs + Noise per Voice

# Moog Muse

## 2024 / £2,999

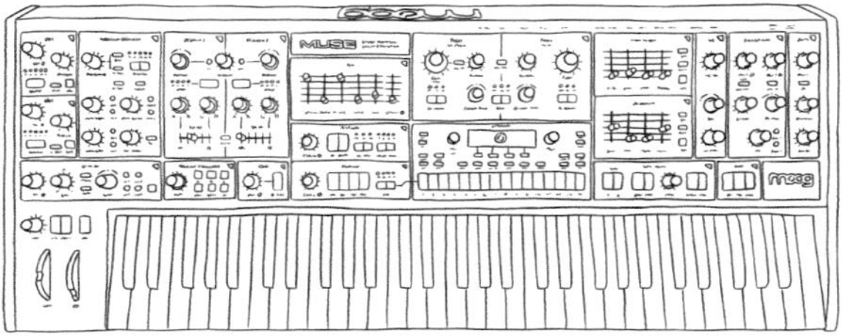


The most recent addition to this volume sees Moog release what could be the next analogue polyphonic classic - a slightly simpler, slightly more affordable Moog One.

Retaining its Moog-y essence, it offers three VCOs per voice (one can be used for modulation or audio), classic Moog ladder filters, FM capabilities, three LFOs, and just enough modern features to satisfy any synthesist in search of 'that sound'.

Analogue / 8 Voice / 3 VCOs + Noise per Voice

# Nonlinear Labs C15

## 2017 / £4,000

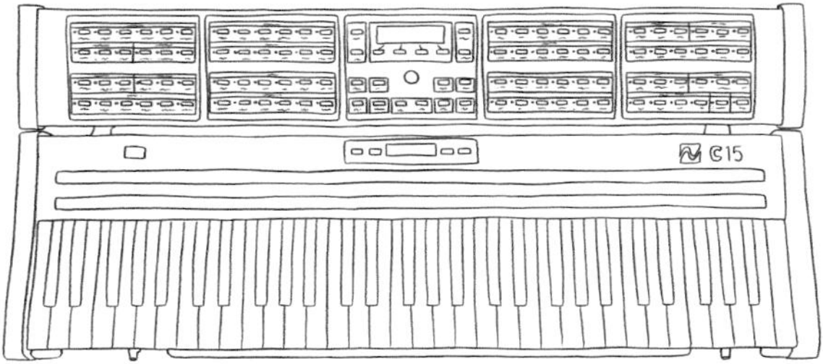


I mean, just look at this beautiful thing! Not only is it ambitious in its looks, it's ambitious in its goal of creating a new type of performance synth. The C15 uses a unique blend of FM and phase distortion that Stephen Schmitt of Nonlinear Labs (and previously of Native Instruments) calls Phase 22.

It generates a different range of sounds to your standard analogue, virtual analogue, wavetable, FM, and ROMpler synths. So confident were Nonlinear Labs in their vision the original C15 didn't even support MIDI...though that was sensibly corrected in later versions.

Digital / 20 Voice / 2 Sound Generators per Voice

# Novation Bass Station II

2013 / £399

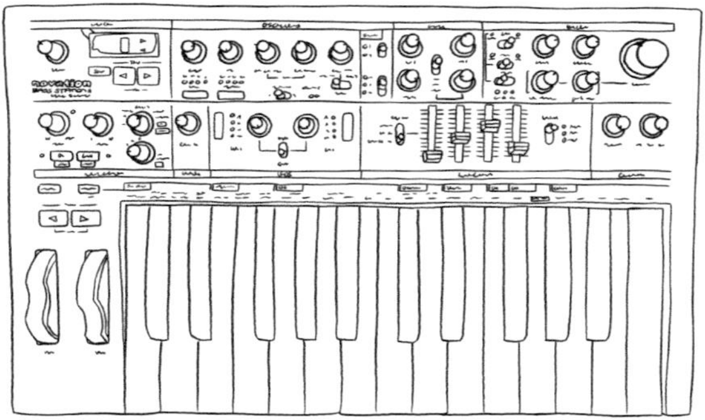

The original Bass Station was an instant hit in 1993, putting Novation firmly on the synth map - and their follow-up, the Supernova, was no slouch either.

Fast forward twenty years, and the Bass Station 2 arrives—not just a rehash but a major upgrade. It features a sturdier chassis, improved knobs, oscillator sync, an arpeggiator, sequencer, and best of all, an additional 'Acid' filter, alongside the 'classic' original by Chris Huggett (EDP Wasp, OSCar, Akai S1000).

Analogue / Monophonic / 2 DCOs

# Novation Summit

## 2019 / £1,899

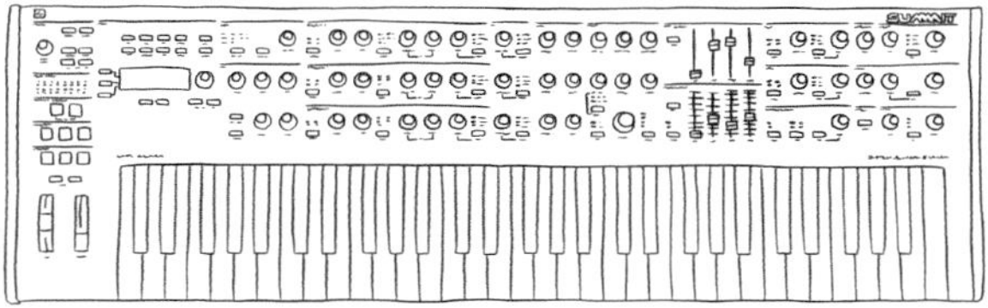

The Peak was Novation's flagship synth of 2017, and the Summit is therefore a kind of double flagship with twin Peaks in the box doubling the polyphony and enabling bi-timbrality. Also new is an additional filter and access to the FM parameters from front surface knobs.

Chris Huggett brings his trademark 'Numerically Controlled Oscillators' (NCOs) to the party, resulting in a powerful, flexible digital synth that soars far above the original Peak.

Digital / 16 Voice / 2 NCOs per Voice

# Oberheim OB-X8

2022 / £4,799

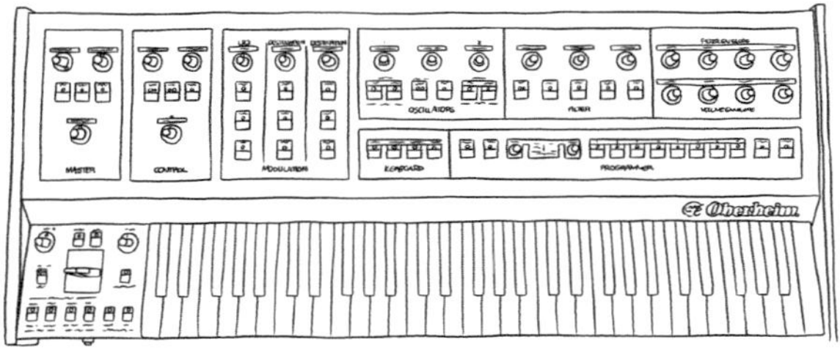

Oberheim are back! Tom Oberheim worked with Sequential to bring back the sound of the revered OB series - the OB-X (1979), OB-SX (1980), OB-Xa (1981), and the OB-8 (1983).

Based on SEM/OB-X lineage VCOs and SEM-lineage VCFs and genuine Curtis filters, this magnificent beast can accurately recreate the sound of all these classic synths at a fraction of the cost of a second-hand original (if you could even find one!).

Analogue / 8 Voice / 2 Osc per Voice

# Roland Jupiter-X

## 2020 / £2,199

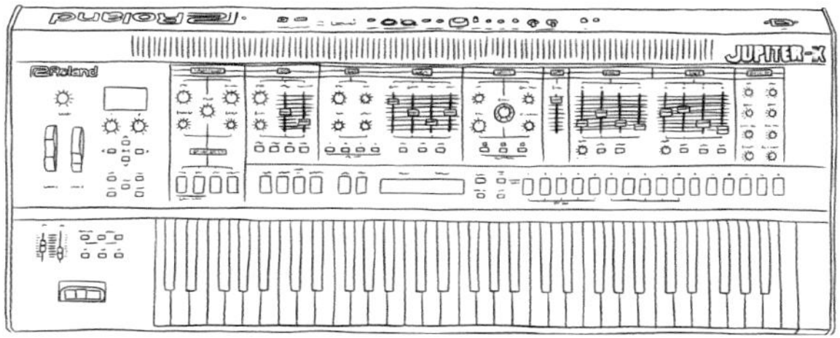


Resolutely refusing to enter the analogue re-release game like so many of their American counterparts, Roland is determined to continue to Design The Future according to today's technology (even if they can't help but invoke the ancient and sacred name of 'Jupiter').

However, the Jupiter-X does offer modern virtual analogue recreations of the Jupiter 8, Juno 106, Super-JX10, and SH-101 - but with better reliability and vastly more polyphony. A pretty good option, I'd say.

Virtual Analogue / 64 Voice / 4 Partials per Voice

# Roland V-Synth

## 2007 / £2,114

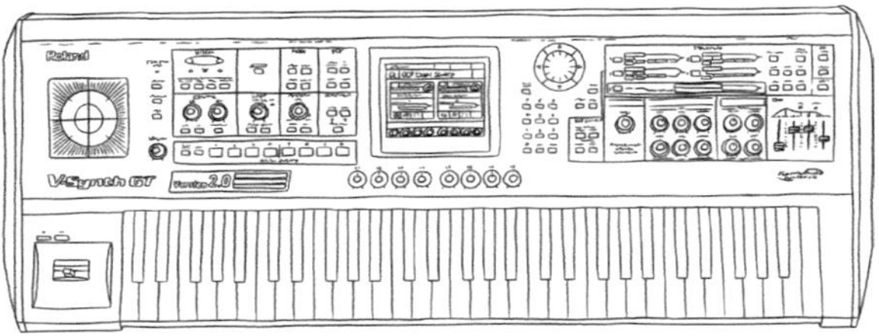

A valiant pre-MPE attempt to equip players with as many expressive controls as possible taking advantage of Roland's advanced sample processing technologies: 'Composite Object Sound Modeling' (COSM) and 'Articulative Phrase Synthesis' (APS).

Using twin D-Beams, a 'Time Trip' pad, pedal inputs, velocity input, aftertouch sensitivity and Roland's signature pitch/modulation waggler™, players could shape sounds in real-time across multiple dimensions.

Sample & Synthesis / 28 Voice / 2 Tones per Patch

# Schmidt Eightvoice Polyphonic Synthesizer

2013 / €19,900

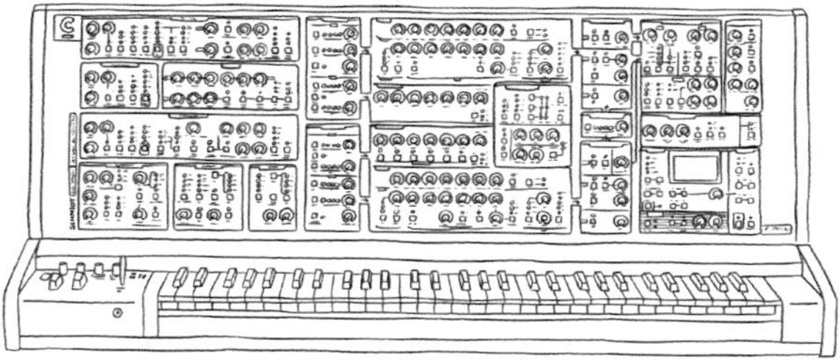

The Eightvoice is by Schmidt's own admission a 'no compromise' analogue polyphonic synthesizer - with a price tag to match. Proudly stating that all sound generation circuitry is discrete (no voices-on-a-chip here), each voice comprises three fully specified analogue oscillators and an extra digital oscillator for complex waves.

Sound sculpting includes three multi-mode filters, multi-PWM, multi-ring modulation, and extensive modulation routings for the best of what 2013 analogue technology could muster - which was ... a lot!

Analogue / 8 Voice / 4 Osc per Voice

# Studio Electronics Omega 8

## 2004 / £3,999

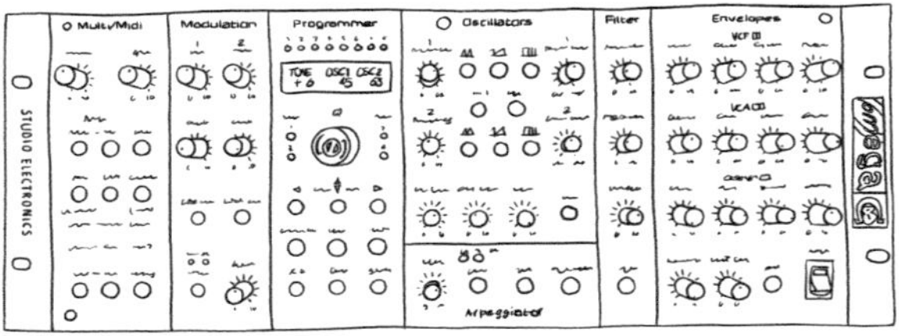


A true eight voice analogue synth - albeit with digital control - the Studio Electronics Omega 8 is a worthy addition to the pantheon of classic eight voice analogue polyphonic synthesizers. Its software is reputed to be a bit buggy - but the sound is immense.

Can be used as an eight-note polyphonic synth or as eight separate monosynths, thanks to the individual inputs and outputs for each voice card.

Analogue / 8 Voice / 2 Osc + Sub + Noise per Voice

# Synclavier Regen

## 2023 / £2,599

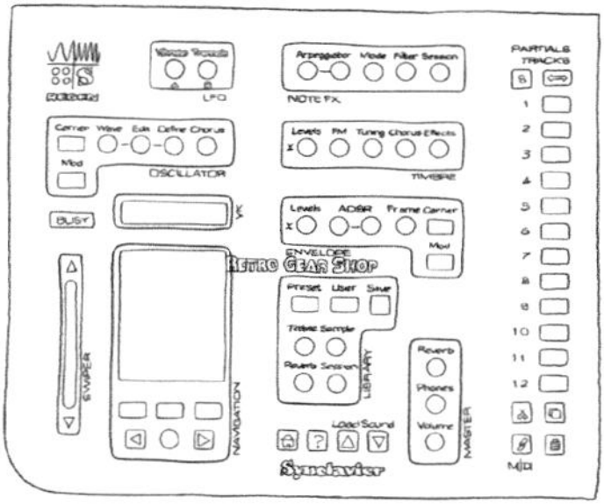


Another 80s machine made from pure unobtanium is resurrected for the modern era!

Like the original NED Synclavier II, the Regen is a deep programming experience, using paradigms of FM, additive synthesis and sample resynthesis... i.e., it's not an analogue synth with a big fat filter knob! (And neither does it replicate the pure sampling or digital multitrack studio aspects of the Synclavier system).

And it comes in at a tiny fraction of the original's $148,000 list price for the model 9600!

Additive, FM & Sample Resynthesis / 98 Voice
2 Partials per Voice

# Teenage Engineering OP-1

2011 / €799

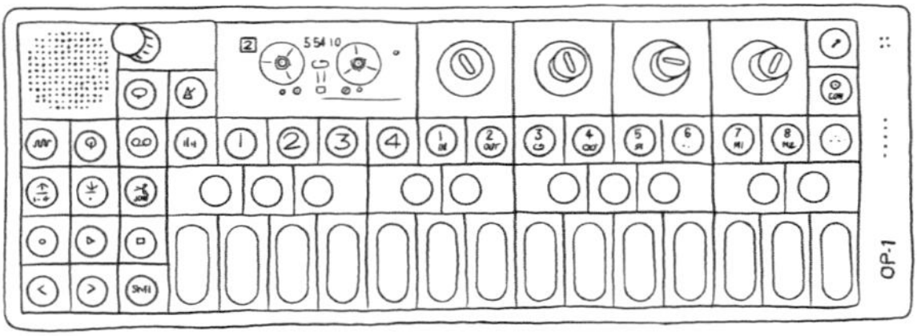


Teenage Engineering burst onto the scene in 2011 with their hotly anticipated OP1. A breath of fresh air, the OP1 offered portable sequencing and synthesis in a way not seen before (or, at least, not since the Casio VL-1!)

Eight types of synthesis make this a very versatile box: FM, Sampler, String Model, Cluster (a kind of supersaw), Digital, Pulse Wave, Dr Wave (frequency domain synthesis), and Phase Distortion.

Coupled with an immediacy designed to capture the Muse while inspiration lasts (via some quirky sequencer options), Teenage Engineering went on to release the well-regarded Pocket Operator series, and…a mediaeval synth. Don't ask.

Digital / 6 Voice / Variable Osc per Voice

# UDO Audio Super Gemini

2024 / £3,595

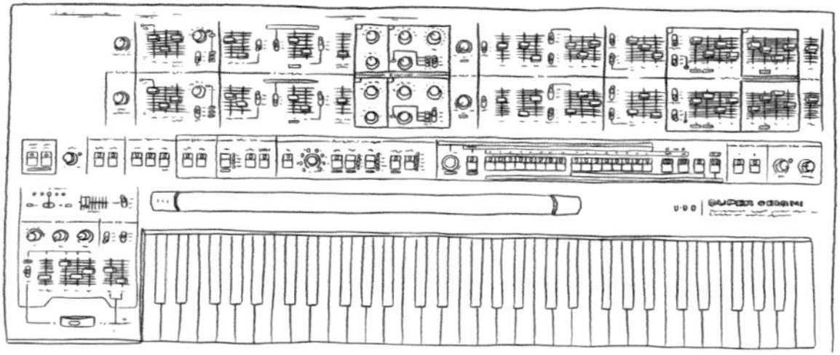

The Super Gemini's name harks back to the golden age of space-named synths - the Roland Jupiter 8, proMars and Saturn, Moog Satellite, Novation Supernova, and the Alesis Andromeda. Spaciness is just always the future, right?

The Super Gemini is UDO's flagship synth, which is more than just two Super 6s in a box (though that does explain the duplicate rows of controls on the front panel and the allusion to twins in the name). New is the ability to morph waveforms and a rather exciting ribbon controller for even more performance versatility.

Virtual Analogue / 20 voice
2 'Direct Digital Synthesis' Osc per Voice

# Vermona Perfourmer

## 2003 / £649

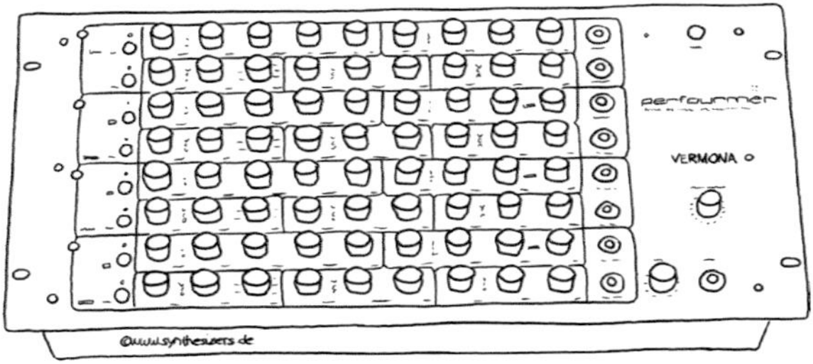


A highly regarded mono/duo/four-note polyphonic synth. At first glance the Perfourmer may not seem to offer anything too special - four mono oscillators with the expected filter/envelope/modulation signal path (albeit with FM), but (and this is important) - it sounds gorgeous. And that's all you need to know really!

(A mkII was released in 2012 which added more waveforms to the oscillators, and oscillator sync).

Analogue / Mono/Duo/4 Voice / 4 Osc

# Waldorf Blofeld

## 2008 / £349

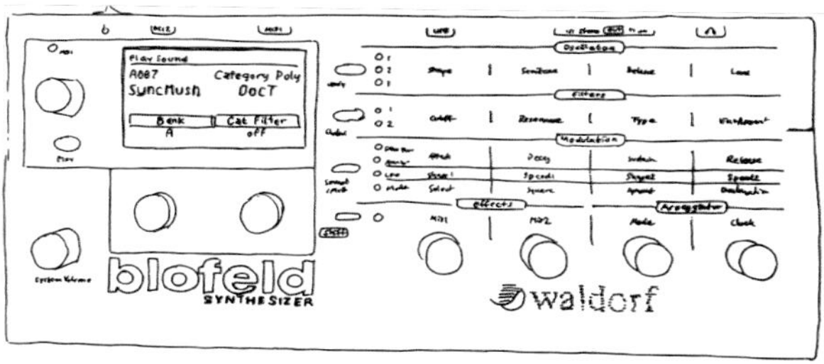


After very nearly going extinct, Waldorf managed to make a comeback with the Bond-villain-inspired Blofeld synth.

It comes loaded with the best wavetables of the Microwave 2, the 'Q' (more Bond!) - and the PPG Wave.

At this price and with this level of polyphony, gaining access to all the classic Waldorf and PPG sounds is a heist most Bond villains could only dream of.

Wavetable/FM/Virtual Analogue / 25 Voice / 3 Osc per Voice

# Yamaha Motif 7

## 2001 / £2,000

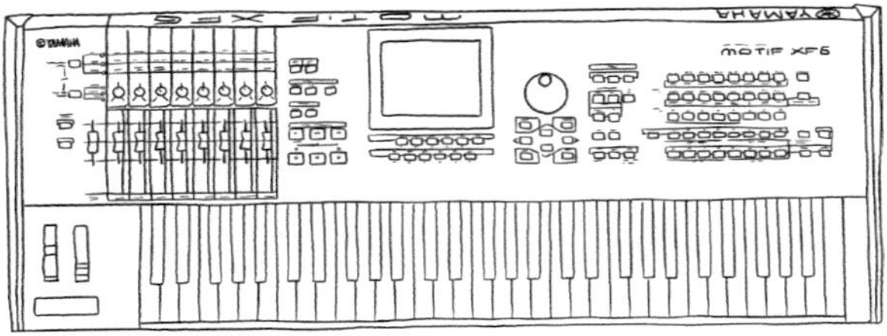


A highly respected keyboard marking the start of the Motif workstation series, the Motif 7 provided the working musician with all the sounds, drums, effects and sequencing required for an original take on ‘in the box’ production.

Built around Yamaha’s proven sample & synthesis technology (‘Advanced Wave Memory 2’), it was expandable through the use of voice cards to add additional sound engines: FM, piano/harpsichord, physical modelling, acoustic modelling and effects/harmoniser.

AWM2 & Sampling / 62 Voice / 4 AWM2 Osc per Voice

# Yamaha Montage 7

## 2017 / £2,985

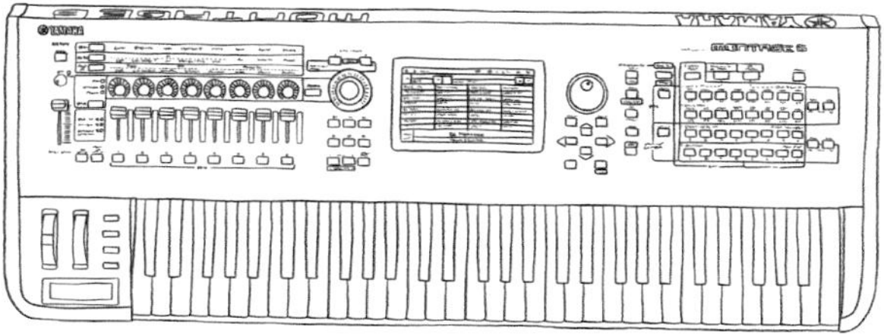

The Montage 7 is an impressive digital synthesizer - not workstation - that provides vast amounts of polyphony from its two built-in synth engines which extend both the sample & synthesis of AWM2 and Yamaha's original FM in the form of 'FM-X'. The Montage 6 and 8 were virtually identical but had different keyboard specs.

Not all classics need to have authentic analogue VCOs, VCFs and VCAs!

AWM2 & FM-X / 256 Voice / 8 'Elements' per Part

First published by **Velocity Press 2025**

velocitypress.uk
synthevolution.net



All illustrations
**Oli Freke**

Design
**Banana Gun**



VP049

ISBN: 978-1-913231-72-9